Post your finished work and join the community.
#FAITHINCOLOR

A GRATEFUL HEART

ADULT COLORING BOOK

COLOR and Give Thanks for God's Abundant Provisions

PASSIO

We give thanks to God and the Father of our Lord

Jesus Christ, praying always for you.

—COLOSSIANS 1:3, MEV

Rest in His Grace

It is easy to be swept away in the daily current of life. You might be busy making plans for the next week or the next month, and become so focused on the future that you don't realize you are not taking the time to focus on the present—much less be thankful for it. If you've had a bad day, week, or month, feeling grateful is a difficult emotion. But a bad moment does not equate to a bad life. God is with us through the good and the bad. He leans down to listen to our prayers. He wants you to spend time with Him so that He can provide you with an abundance of love and peace.

Our intention is that as you color, you will reflect on the day—good or bad—and remember that God is in complete control. Perhaps you didn't see it at the time, but looking back, you are now able to thank Him for His faithfulness. Record these memories in this book or a journal. Praising God for His faithfulness will build your faith, helping you believe that He is able to meet every need that you face now or in your future. You can trust Him and continue to praise Him. And when you do, His peace, "which surpasses all understanding, will protect your hearts and minds through Christ Jesus" (Phil. 4:7).

We've placed these carefully selected verses from Scripture on the facing page of each design. Each one was chosen to complement the illustration while inspiring you to lift your own praises to God with a grateful heart. As you color these designs, reflect quietly on God's goodness and the many gifts He has bestowed upon you. When you are encouraged by God's promises to love and care for you, you will find that the cares and worries of life melt away.

It might interest you to know that the verses in this book are taken from the Modern English Version of the Holy Bible. The Modern English Version (MEV) is the most modern translation produced in the King James tradition within the last thirty years. This formal equivalence translation maintains the beauty of the past yet provides fresh clarity for a new generation of Bible readers. If you would like more information on the MEV, please visit www.mevbible.com.

We hope you find this coloring book to be both beautiful and inspirational. As you color, remember that the best artistic endeavors have no rules. Unleash your creativity as you experiment with colors, textures, and mediums. Freedom of self-expression will help to release wellness, balance, mindfulness, and inner peace into your life, allowing you to enjoy the process as well as the finished product. When you're finished, you can frame your favorite creations for displaying or gift giving. Then post your artwork on Facebook, Twitter, or Instagram with the hashtag #FAITHINCOLOR.

I thank and praise You, O God of my fathers;

for You have given me wisdom and might.

—Daniel 2:23, MEV

The LORD is my Strength my Shield

—Psalm 28:7

In God we boast all the day long,

and give thanks to Your name forever.

—Psalm 44:8, MEV

I will praise the name of God with a song,

and will magnify Him with thanksgiving.

—P<small>SALM</small> 69:30, <small>MEV</small>

Now thanks be to God who always causes us

to triumph in Christ and through us reveals the

fragrance of His knowledge in every place.

—2 Corinthians 2:14, MEV

All these things are for your sakes, so that the

abundant grace through the thanksgiving of many

might overflow to the glory of God.

—2 CORINTHIANS 4:15, MEV

In everything give thanks, for this is the will of God

in Christ Jesus concerning you.

—*1 Thessalonians 5:18,* MEV

In everything GIVE THANKS for this is the will of God

1 THESSALONIANS 5:18

For by grace you have been saved through faith,

and this is not of yourselves. It is the gift of God,

not of works, so that no one should boast.

—Ephesians 2:8–9, MEV

We have all received from His fullness grace upon grace.

—*John 1:16,* MEV

But as you abound in everything—in faith, in utterance, in knowledge, in all diligence, and in your love to us—see that you abound in this grace also.

—2 Corinthians 8:7, MEV

Let your speech always be with grace, seasoned with salt,

that you may know how you should answer everyone.

—COLOSSIANS 4:6, MEV

The grace of our Lord overflowed with the

faith and love which is in Christ Jesus.

—1 Timothy 1:14, MEV

But after you have suffered a little while, the God of all grace, who has called us to His eternal glory through Christ Jesus, will restore, support, strengthen, and establish you.

—*1 Peter 5:10,* MEV

*Know that the L*ORD *set apart the faithful for*

*Himself; the L*ORD *hears when I call to Him.*

*—P*SALM *4:3,* MEV

the LORD set apart the Faithful for HIMSELF

—Psalm 4:3

For Your mercy is great above the heavens;

Your faithfulness reaches to the clouds.

—PSALM 108:4, MEV

For His merciful kindness is great toward us,

and the faithfulness of the LORD endures forever.

—PSALM 117:2, MEV

the faithfulness of the LORD endures forever.

Psalm 117:2

*"The L*ORD *is my portion," says my soul,*

"therefore I will hope in Him."

*—L*AMENTATIONS *3:24,* MEV

Let us firmly hold the profession of our faith without

wavering, for He who promised is faithful.

—HEBREWS 10:23, MEV

Be faithful unto death,

and I will give you the crown of life.

—REVELATION 2:10, MEV

Patience produces character,

and character produces hope.

—Romans 5:4, MEV

You will trust because there is hope; yes, you will search about you, and you will look around and rest in safety.

—JOB 11:18, MEV

Let Your lovingkindness, O LORD, be

on us, just as we hope in You.

—PSALM 33:22, MEV

Let your lovingkindness, O Lord,

be on us, just as we hope in you.

—PSALM 33:22

On the day I called, You answered me,

and strengthened me in my soul.

—Psalm 138:3, MEV

The Lord will fulfill His purpose for me;

Your mercy, O Lord, endures forever.

—Psalm 138:8, MEV

the LORD will fulfill His purpose for me

Psalm 138:8

Give thanks always for all things to God the Father

in the name of our Lord Jesus Christ.

—*EPHESIANS 5:20, MEV*

Enter into His gates with thanksgiving, and into His courts

with praise; be thankful to Him, and bless His name.

—PSALM 100:4, MEV

Let the peace of God, to which also you are called in one body,

rule in your hearts. And be thankful.

—COLOSSIANS 3:15, MEV

So now, do not fear. I will provide

for you and your little ones.

—Genesis 50:21, MEV

For in this way the entrance into the eternal

kingdom of our Lord and Savior Jesus Christ

will be abundantly provided for you.

—2 Peter 1:11, MEV

For I will restore health to you,

and I will heal you of your wounds, says the Lord.

—Jeremiah 30:17, MEV

If we have food and clothing, we shall be content with these things.

1 TIMOTHY 6:8

He who dwells in the shelter of the Most High

shall abide under the shadow of the Almighty.

—Psalm 91:1, MEV

In God is my salvation and my glory; the rock of my

strength, and my shelter, is in God.

—PSALM 62:7, MEV

For God so loved the world that He gave His only begotten Son, that whoever believes in Him should not perish, but have eternal life. For God did not send His Son into the world to condemn the world, but that the world through Him might be saved.

—JOHN 3:16–17, MEV

The fruit of the Spirit is love, joy, peace, patience, gentleness, goodness, faith, meekness, and self-control.

—GALATIANS 5:22–23, MEV

Do not be grieved,

*for the joy of the L*ord *is your strength.*

*—N*ehemiah *8:10,* mev

But may all those who seek refuge in You rejoice;

may they ever shout for joy, because You defend them;

may those who love Your name be joyful in You.

—Psalm 5:11, MEV

Then I will go to the altar of God, to the God

of my joyful gladness; with the harp I will

give thanks to You, O God, my God.

—Psalm 43:4, MEV

Most CHARISMA HOUSE BOOK GROUP products are available at special quantity discounts for bulk purchase for sales promotions, premiums, fund-raising, and educational needs. For details, write Charisma House Book Group, 600 Rinehart Road, Lake Mary, Florida 32746, or telephone (407) 333-0600.

A GRATEFUL HEART published by Passio
Charisma Media/Charisma House Book Group
600 Rinehart Road
Lake Mary, Florida 32746
www.charismahouse.com

Design Director: Justin Evans
Cover Design: Justin Evans
Interior Design: Justin Evans, Lisa Rae McClure, Vincent Pirozzi

Illustrations: Getty Images/Depositphotos

International Standard Book Number: 978-1-62998-964-8

First edition

16 17 18 19 20 — 987654321

Printed in the United States of America